Sidelines

Joy always...

Sidelines

Peter Hrastovec

Black Moss Press

2015

Library and Archives Canada Cataloguing in Publication

Hrastovec, Peter, author
        Sidelines / Peter Hrastovec.

Poems.

ISBN 978-0-88753-545-1 (pbk.)

        I. Title.

PS8615.R38S53 2015   C811'.6   C2015-900531-0

Cover Image by: Amber Dilabbio

Edited by: Jaylyn Bernachi, Julian Del Bel Belluz, Angie Desaulniers, Amber
Dilabbio, Wesley Foster, Julianne Lacroix, Ola Raniszewska, Rachel Reed,
Amber Shearer, Sofia Tesic, Jay Rankin, Shawna Partridge

Published by Black Moss Press at 2450 Byng Road, Windsor, Ontario, N8W
3E8, Canada. Black Moss books are distributed in Canada and the US by
Fitzhenry & Whiteside. All orders should be directed there. Black Moss
Press books can also be found on our website blackmosspress.com.

Printed in Canada.    Black Moss
                                                    Press

Black Moss Press would like to acknowledge the support of the Canada
Council for the Arts and the Ontario Arts Council for their support of its
publishing program.

For my 'coach and confidante' Denise,
and for my Andrea, Stephen, and Aaron—my team,
my ubiquitous joy!

Make each day your masterpiece
—John Wooden

ACKNOWLEDGEMENTS

So it began something like this:

Over a hearty breakfast of coffee, eggs and hash browns laced with onions at our usual haunt, friend and poet, Marty Gervais convinces me that my very next book should be edited by his *Editing & Publishing team* at the University of Windsor. With a sales pitch for the ages, he tells me how my writing has "grown" and that my work and personality will fit with this program. He tells me how I will get to work with a group of enterprising publishing interns, and that it will allow me to get back to the University of Windsor campus regularly, a place that, throughout my adult life, has invigorated me with every visit. Before I down a second cup of coffee, I have accepted this deal. A good idea, or so I am told by Windsor's poet laureate.

What I came to realize pretty quickly was that it was more than a good idea—it was a great idea. But it didn't start well for me. A mid-summer computer crash left me without a manuscript and my "real job" and the vagaries of daily living got in the way. Through a minor miracle (and the fact that as a digital pack rat, I had duplicate copies located on three different computers plus notes and handwritten versions), I managed to piece together a manuscript before the fall session began. My text then found its way into the hands of a zealous group of Marty's young editors. I didn't know them and they, certainly, didn't know anything about me. Feeling somewhat paranoid and exposed, I envisioned that they would begin to dissect my manuscript as if it was a laboratory frog—some gleefully, others exhibiting disgust and all prone to biting sarcasm and a "let's get this over with" mentality. Talk about intrusive!

Of course, nothing was further from the truth. They handled my work with care. As I write this piece, I realise how much I owe those who, despite their youth (or perhaps because of it), kept me on pace, challenged my thinking, debated simple phrasing, argued over punctuation, imagery, titles, word usage, questioned my rationale for writing certain pieces, probed with curiosity my love of sports, told me that I talked too much, pondered and questioned my list of favourite authors and books—yeah, you can say, they exhausted me! But in the end, I am left with this feeling of exhilaration, this sense of excitement that the project achieved what we both expected. I learned something about this program, unique to the University of Windsor and the collaborative process that taught me much about who I am as a poet and a writer, while giving a group of clever and creative interns a work in progress to shape into a published book. In the end, this most humbling experience spawned a book built on trust while providing me with a profound sense of gratitude for having this chance to work with a group of diligent interns. It was a learning experience and I was "schooled".

So to the team—Rachel Reed, Julian Del Bel Belluz, Ola Raniszewska, Angie Desaulniers, Amber Dilabbio, Amber Shearer, Sofia Tesic, Julianne Lacroix, Wes Foster and Jaylyn Bernachi—a hearty thank you. Admittedly they did this for credit; I did it to get another book published. But through their unsullied efforts, I ended up with a whole lot more. I had the better deal.

Some of these poems have appeared in anthologies—the *Windsor Review, Whiskey Sour City, Glimpse*—to name but a few. The rest are either new works, older poems that have been reworked and things that didn't quite fit thematically in my first book, *In Lieu of Flowers*. Thankfully, my first editor, the discerning Marie Jeanette, had the wisdom and insight to hold back on some and they appear here for the first time. Though she was not directly involved in the editing of this book, I do want to thank Marie for some ancillary advice and support in the making of this book.

Thanks as well to the Department of English at the University of Windsor, my old stomping grounds, for allowing me to "stomp" once more.

And many thanks to the graphic design folks, the marketing gurus and the rest of Marty's crew who, in one way or another, participated in this project. In particular, I would like to acknowledge Amber Dilabbio whose original painting was chosen as the cover for this book. I also offer a shout out to Amber Shearer for her Photoshop skills in the final design.

I feel fortunate to be able to do something of this magnitude because I have an understanding and supportive soulmate in my Denise, my best friend and most ardent critic of my writing and of my life generally. Like a good coach, she keeps me "in the game".

If you have read this much and gotten this far, I can only hope that you will read a little more. Your support is treasured.

PETER HRASTOVEC
Walkerville, Ontario
2015

Contents

IMMIGRANT

borne on the back of a distant dream
i came to this country
(or should i say that this country came to me?)

ankles soaked by Atlantic swill
my father ached his way across
this bread and butter landscape
with a tongue weighted down by ignorance
but with a spirit that spoke survival

and my mother followed in the blind procession
her shining star tarnished by a decade of sorrows
dragged into a post-war promised land
with only the assurance of a daughter's warm hand

while i rumbled
intrusively in darkness
like the darkening ocean's prophetic lament

STOLEN BASES

—*to all my friends from Mitchell Park*

underfoot
the grass was luxurious
weaving a carpet of comfort
damp and cool
between our bare toes

endless afternoons
of shagging baseballs
in the bold summer sun
that lit up the day
like a thousand ballpark lamps

we would run for hours
hot box between the bases
mimicking our heroes
their bold stance at the plate
their wide-eyed major league grins
staring down pitchers
leaning into a slider
running safely
to home plate
to score

where i once drove in runs
i now drive by
the field that
governed my summers
the space that was
bigger than anything
i had ever known

i now take the bench
my heart a tattered jersey
my spirit a splintered bat

i search for signs
of the life i knew
in an empty field
that once played home
to a collection of
big league wannabes
dusty and dishevelled dreamers

there is only the grass and goalposts
backstop infield benches
gone, vanished like a ball to the bleachers
i throw a phantom knuckler toward
a backstop that no longer exists
no, not even a place to sit
and ride the pines remains

"kids play soccer now"
says the parks official
"so we remove the hardware
and fill in with grass"
he turns and walks away
like a disgruntled manager
heading back to the dugout
having made his point

i am left lamenting
my sore pitching arm
the slow eradication of my youth
and the dismantling of dream fields
those sacred and hallowed grounds

where steel-eyed youngsters
with ratty gloves and well-worn spikes
would live like the kings of summer
in a time when a called third strike
was the absolute worst thing
that could happen

besides rain

ONE AFTERNOON OUT WALKING

"I protest!"

"I protest!"

declared the old man
in the grey flannel suit
war medals jingling
on his worn lapel

"I protest!"

white hair whiter beard
pasty face and weathered fedora
a chipped walking cane that
knew many miles

"I protest!"

marching marching
alone and in time
through crowds
gawking awkwardly

brushing past us
pushing past us
a neo-Santa with purpose

"I protest!"

he shouts again
and again with aging
lungs and nostrils
flaring and mouth
clenched tight and
menacing enough
to frighten children

"I protest!"

he roars
waking the dead

within minutes his "I protest" is
a whimper
a car door slammed
a child whining
a distant plane overhead
an afterthought
an old photograph
a distorted sound
a muffled memory

i watch as he hunches over
in the distance
hunches to clutch over
a pocket watch
or some loose change
or perhaps to see
how the lines
on the palm
of his hand
have become drawn

"what does he protest?"
i asked my father

"the same as everyone else"
my father answers

leaving the man

and me

out

in the street

ADRIATIC MATINS

in my mother's village
the church stands
at the top
of the hill
its white-washed walls
stripped shamelessly by
the indelicate touch
of briny winds
while immodest windows
wrench themselves
free from casements cracked with age

the old grey clock
numbed into stubborn silence
wears an embarrassed grin
and stares blindly out to sea
the small gothic steeple
the triumph of some
deceased generation
points an indignant finger
at the innocent morning
breaking in blue

and far, far below
beneath this ancient peace
an army of old women
parading in their best black
undertake their private pilgrimages
and collect like dust
under the foot
of this bloodless calvary

brandishing prayers unsheathed
in strategic anticipation
of one united assault
on God

rumour has it
he's resting

REMEMBRANCE DAY

this tall guy
with medals on his jacket
glistening like the polished
silver of his hair

stands up and tells
the most amazing story
about liberating Holland

with a sten gun that jammed
and a fearless defiance that took prisoners
on a day his friends and sergeant

took the short trip to paradise
leaving him to clean up and bug out
just to tell us a few war stories

i remember the gleam in his eye
as i shook his trembling hand
thanking him for courage
inspired by fear
tempered by adventure

and i wonder
about stolen youth
miscalculated ordinances
mistakes made
all belonging to a time
of grave decisions
and choices made
by those who can
never remember

ever lost like shell casings
in the mud
trampled underfoot

undermined and
rarely understood

DOCUMENTARY

Benito Mussolini was hung by his heels
along with his mistress both having been
shot by the same people who once saluted
them

DUCE, DUCE, DUCE

some may call this overkill but in truth
they die three times a week
restrung in the same plaza
in a video
that replays itself
on the history channel
the documentary channel
the capital death channel
or whatever channel
shows this stuff
with continuing repetition
(television's purgatory)

i complain that my children
do not watch enough
documentaries but
i am squeamish about this one
and other such capital acts
horrors and pestilence
crammed between commercials

i shoo my son outside to play ball
"be a kid" i say
there will be time
enough for documentaries

saving these
black and white shadows
for the sudden loss
of innocence

looming just
around the corner
or less remotely
just a click
or two away

WATERFIGHT

there are no rules
in guerilla warfare

no room
for fair play

take no prisoners
and paybacks are

a bit out of
the ordinary

in the mind of
a five-year-old

with a vacuum pump
water gun that shoots

fifty feet of ego-bruising fun
no truces no treaties

no reparations
no negotiations

only the wakening
blast of cold water

coupled with
a sinister laugh

both chilling
to the bone

DAVID IN NEED OF A TAILOR

—without apologizing to Michelangelo

this penchant for sculpting nudes
intended to satisfy some primordial
predisposition and delight

did it not occur to you
that the sight of him
would spark the jeers of
school-aged children

rush the blood of romantics
and cause many men to question
why they shouldn't frequent the

nearest gym

in search of a body

built by time?

MENTOR

—for L.

the teacher in you
told tales of the street
how to survive a bloodless war
how to fill the coffers
to the brim with the spoils of battle

such was your booty
the wages of sin were not easily forgotten
and the prisoners you took were
freed up for another day

how soon you forgot
who you were
fumbling for identification
while we held up mirrors
for you to see that
you really were
still here with us
still here for us

and when you finally left
we chose to remember
the early you
our hearts though stung
remained open awaiting
the prodigal's return

like frost

in your farmer's field

REGRETS

i will blame
a healthy fear
of bears

and a news story
about a woman
surviving an attack

by feeding her arm
inch by gnawing inch
until the bear was stuffed

and you
fearless and inspired
by wine cheese and desire
in this wild and untamed state
this forest green with growing ardour

wanting much and expecting more
left failing to undo my hamstrung heart
with passion's imperfect timing

and me fumbling
with clothing fright and panic
juggling horrors so potent
of circus bears and hapless clowns
and chance left dangling

like a half-chewed arm
or an opportunity lost

in the woods

DAYDREAM

screen door snapping shut
startles the hide-and-seek birds
their squawking
breaking morning's recurring silence

like a soccer referee
signaling a foul
the shrill whistle of one bird
summons me
from the swill
of my second coffee

i breathe
my summer mantra
is the cool crisp air
filtering through
every open window
inviting every
waking breath

i float high
above the island
winged like a bird or
one of Da Vinci's
intricate drawings
of man-made flight
i rise faster
and fly farther
than Icarus
beaming with brilliant
sunlight like some
lesser known saint

turning to take in the view
and feeling the harsh
cold thud of a floor
meant to break my fall

having slipped
from the chair
my tumble into
the harsh waking
cruelty of a day
marked by the
blatant boredom
of chores and
ego-bruising
clumsiness

steeped
and filled
to the brim

BAJAN VILLAGE

greeted by tangy odours
of lazy rum-drinkers sizzling
in sun after sun after
village woman with load on head
squeezes foaming fat
between fast cars
and no curb
and old disease on one leg
wants to buy your change
with his fish
you turn to see
little brown boy
peering from ruined hut
at the promise of tomorrow
jingling sunlight
in your naked palm

HANDCHECK

rush of passengers
rushing through the terminal
rushing for a plane
running to the gate

slowing down for security
lifting bag to conveyor
baring a carry-on's soul
to x-rays most intrusive

walking through the scanner
i am not a threat
i am not a danger
but become a suspect by
a beep of detection

a metal pin mostly forgotten
as useful or as useless
as a button and
the only reason
my hands now
tremble

BLOOD STONES

—Dieppe Park, August 19, 2012

on a waterfront
on a perfect afternoon
children eat ice cream
chase balloons
pets and siblings
families picnic
cyclists glide and
couples saunter past
hand-in-hand

almost unnoticed
the dedicated gather
at a monument
of remembrance
to watch kilt-wearing cadets
and resplendent soldiers
march past decorated veterans
sitting guard
sentinels in wheelchairs
drummers' pulse
and pipers' lament
fill the sky and
break the silence
intended for
absent comrades

prayers are offered
speeches shared
and wreaths gently
placed with pride

in this space
meant for peace

calmly
the congregation
begin their exit
some remain behind
to bend
and touch the base
of this pristine plinth
gritty stones packed
in concrete and sorrow
unearthed
from a foreign beach
without children
ice cream or lovers
placed on this site
in their bloodless state
far from the carnage
and the horror
washed clean
by incessant tides

stones placed here
with deep and
abiding reverence
a sober and gentle reminder
that pain is a fossil
of the heart
left for others
to discover

HOW HUNGRY CAN WE BE?

a size fifty suit on shoulders
that used to scare my mother
because she could not believe
that something so big could
have once been inside her

i go to the photo album to remind
her that it took years of careful preparation
training and dedication to get this big
and, oh yes, the propensity to over-eat

never mind she says
it's time to stay away
from the fridge
read a book and let starvation
become the way
a noble truth
for which a
joyous trip
to the tailor
will be the
ultimate reward

how hungry
can
i be?

enough to wonder
why i chew on pen caps
and would they taste better
with barbeque sauce?

AMENDMENTS

the by-law allows
dogs the freedom
to walk unrestrained
throughout the park
carefree and steps
ahead of their masters
emancipated canines
marching blithely as
if liberated from
the bonds of endless
four-legged servitude

i surmise that
soon they will ask
for the right to vote
to own property
the right to marry
to worship and the choice
to bark up the wrong tree

i view this changing landscape
this dogged willingness
to alter states
to change the rules

in safe seclusion
behind a window
inside and away
far away from

the madding pack

CHARLES DARWIN WEARS
A CUSTOM-MADE SUIT

we are taught to negotiate
to work the room
like a hungry animal
raised on economic survivalist claptrap
hunting for contacts
the next file
fame and immortality
power most unholy
the epitome of
political manifest destinies
all the while
tempted by the passion
exuding from
a pale piece of blue cheese

i fill my glass
and feed my face
and forget for a moment
that this world is a jungle
and i am scavenging

for roots

AND SO IT GOES

the cane-bearing applicant
supplicant to his cause and claim
winces in dramatic pain with every
word the lawyer uses
to describe with meticulous detail
the misfortune of the incident
that changed his life forever

the maladies molded
into a mosaic
of sordid aches and bruises
and failing body parts
broken like the machinery
he once knew
a career that ticked
with clockwork precision
leaving him now
a walking scrap heap
that attracts the sympathy
of cynics and allies alike

and voila a cheque appears
like magic and oh miracle of miracles
the pain disappears as if
a cure is conjured up with every stroke
of the signatures on the settlement papers
every curl of the elegant nom de plume
that signifies his troubles are history
the future secure
and that the life that remains
is summed up
in a government pension

the price that is paid for
being loyal, trustworthy
a boy scout without badges

and so the story goes
how the lame finally walk
how the blind can suddenly see
and how a multitude of other divine acts
are performed daily
on the twenty-seventh floor
of an office building
in a world as surreal
as that of a babbling man
a cane discarded
and the jaded disposition
of a disciple
destined for denial

PRESSURE

this email crazy world
where messages
fill my screen
like carpenter ants

i am a killer of trees
though i could
hardly wield an axe
i am the indirect cause
of the demise of a forest
someone chops
grinds the pulp
fabricates the paper
but i am responsible
for their genocide

the letters mailed
in my name
documents revised as often
as i change my socks
boxes of paper
that end up on a shelf
catalogued and categorised
and left forgotten
between generations

if i should squeeze myself
on to one of these shelves
like a file full of letters
i imagine that i too
would be forgotten

CARRYING THE CARD

the brothers and sisters
cross the road
to get to the other side
chickens with lunch pails

no one wears
work boots anymore
those thick-soled kick-
ass mothers with
steel toes so heavy
even God couldn't tap
dance in them

these ones don't look
the part they just
don't look like labour anymore
dressed more for an afternoon
barbeque or shopping at Costco

if they could only see this crew
the ones that made wildcat strikes
headline news and solidarity part of
the new vocabulary and rand formulas
the law and the pounding of fists and
vitriol the stuff of local lore
the old guard would say "what the hell?
who are these guys?"
(making no allowances for gender)

making no apologies for their opinions
because when you apologize for
your views you may as well

kiss your credibility goodbye

so what of it
what about these
six figure socialists
who don't carry picket signs
who don't cross the street
they get chauffeured and such
get manicured and eat quiche
and act like they just
won the lottery or an Oscar

"well they is sort of"
says the poor bastard
"sort of like royalty
like kings dontcha know"

he says this
as he punches in
like there is no
tomorrow
and guess what
there is no tomorrow
only today
on a line
that moves
only in one
direction
like traffic
on a road
that is
never
crossed

THINKING ABOUT SUPPER

i am thinking about supper
while sitting at my desk
in my office
several kilometers
from my kitchen
wondering how i am going
to get a frozen chicken
to remove itself
from my freezer
thaw itself out
and get itself dressed
for dinner
for five
at seven

send out a fax or an email and
hope that it will comply
with this simple request
without much
fanfare hoopla
or protocol

so i concentrate
recall that i once read
a book on telepathy
for a grade school
science fair project on ESP
open the freezer in a trance-like
state and i
reach in and
retrieve a frozen pizza

all the while planning
next dinner's coup

sans grace

SABBATH

we laugh

at the medieval serf
who observed
one hundred fifteen
holy days

(absurd to those of us
who open briefcases
after Sunday brunch)

still laughing

MANNERS

after the phone call
in the dead
silence of disbelief
that separates the dial tone
from the outrage
i hunt for the logic behind
loving one's neighbour
and remember the advice
given willingly by
one American cousin
that justice is embodied
in an unvarnished axe handle
swung quickly and with contact
defining in its aftermath
the meaning of
sin and retribution
harsh words (you may say)
for nameless
faceless telemarketers

given all this
i am therefore thankful
for call screening
bringing me down to earth
with the groundlings
and assorted cowards
with whom this latter day Thurber
keeps good company

wondering all the while
who disturbs the telemarketers?

DISCOVERIES

it wasn't pretty
the pettiness of it all
two grown men in Armani
acting like petulant children
denying each other the opportunity
to resolve this civil dispute with dignity

the two of you
spent the day
beating each other
over the head
as if with
two-by-fours

like rival soldiers
entrenched in war's muck
each waiting for the other
to make the next move
a game of chess
filling time with boring
solitude in a room that is
a vacuum for narrow thinking
unrequited resolution and
a willingness not to be one-upped?

i sit ever the dispassionate observer
and wait while the two of you
refuse to relent for fear
that a reputation or two will be tarnished

all the while forgetting
that the real reason
you snipe is over

the unpaid bill for lunch

IT'S MARGARET ATWOOD'S BIRTHDAY

—including some forgettable end-rhyme
November 18, 2003

no really it is
i was told this
early this morning
on my way
to a meeting
in my car
in a fog
and without warning

i was told this
as if it were
the most important news
told this by some
radio stranger in whom i trust
told this while the geese
gathered for breakfast
on a river
cut from glass
in a park imitating Eden

told this just before
the next commercial
told this like some
deep dark secret
a broken promise
or a shattered rule
told this only
because someone knew

we are told
not to ask a woman's age
but someone asked Margaret
yes someone did
like defying natural law or
telling a forbidden joke
and letting me in on the punch line

like the Beatles you got older (sixty four)
you have your hair and an island mother
a lab experiment for you and your absent father
he still the teacher and you making notes

'rage Margaret rage not against the dying of the light
rage cuz we know your age on this less than perfect night'
for today it is your birthday and if memory serves me right
i'll remember this day yearly—perhaps not, though i just might!

POSSUM PLAYED

a dead possum
in the middle
of the road
the same carcass
that i found
yesterday
once fresh road kill
now compacted
cartoon-like
flattened
forgotten
barely recognizable
a statistic
a trophy
a discussion
over morning coffee

not that i am
insensitive or boorish
i will leave indifference
to passing motorists
and oblivious lovers
focused on the elsewhere
arousals or destinations

i laughed
as i witnessed
the impromptu memorial
and all of the neighbourhood
varmints and vermin

leaving the warmth of
winter's hibernation
to collect safely
at the side
of the road
to pay their respects
or to attempt their
own tortured journeys
across the busy
and bullied street

I SAW IRVING LAYTON ONCE

i saw Irving Layton once
on a stage in a hall at a mic
reading from his books with
old testament panache

he and Moses
could have done burlesque
and sang and danced
their way into our hearts
done road pictures and
loved the same girl
after girl after girl

but this time he read by himself
the elixir of the gods or whatever deity
was the flavour of this month
ran through his veins and poured out
his forehead the furious perspiration
splashing his pages awash with venom
and vitriol and vexing enigmas
reading the poetry forbidden in
some classes because it sang the songs
of the sirens those nude muses with
whom you should not live without
and with whom you should practise
safe poetry

i saw Irving Layton later
beaten down and dying
the memory of his reading
erased with age

i remembered
him reading
and dreaming
and my believing
that poets do not die
but end up in boxes
in eulogies and in a glass
held high to toast
a life well-lived

more a postscript
more than is ever known
by this or the other
barbarians who utter
his name like the prophet

ancient and conning fate

PICKUP

is it any easier than this
to stand at the back of a pickup
like it is some object of art
or an outdoor bar
leaning against the open loader
swilling beer and telling stories
these guys wearing baseball caps
pulled tight over eye brows
the storytellers lending themselves to anonymity

telling stories that will be told retold
told again and again and
never published
stories that outlive
the storytellers
the beer
and the truck
that will in time
lie in a heap
in a landfill
or be recycled
for its parts
like the stories
told

altered and reusable
somewhat useful
but nothing
to write home about

the cycle
repeats itself
the stories retold

like recycled empties

and this too

is expected

ADVICE

it's all about them
and the others
never about us
though it should be

yeah i know
i know it is there
over and over

it's all there
the reasons why
i've kept bad company
the feeling is mutual
it's mutual i say

i cough and hack
and spit up sins
that stick in my throat
and constrict and choke

and still i shudder at the thought
that the last mortal act that i'll
do has less redeeming
qualities than voting

the last act
the thing
that we all do
even in death
the sad inevitability
of life's final duty

a tax return filed
as we turn cold

DINNER AT THE ANCHOR AND WHEEL

—Pelee Island

three beers
into the meal
the conversation
continues like this
"i never met a piece
of pickerel i didn't like"
when without fear
provocation or warning
papa Hemingway
makes his way to my table
bottle and shot glasses in hand
he sits down (no invitation needed)
pouring and proclaiming
over dulcet tones
of Jimmy Buffetting Bob Marley
that he has come to correct
all the misconceptions
of his much maligned
and myth-laden life
and that he'd be damned
double-damned
if he didn't take up
most of the evening
and part of the next day
to state his case
so i should really give up
any fool notion
of trying my hand at fishing
and just sit back and soak up

the stories and swill he'd share
no matter how stretched far-fetched
or sordid it all sounds

and there in the fish-tackled tangle
of seafaring paraphernalia
festooning this island diner
a nautical museum
masquerading as
a popular eatery
forever caught in the hurricane's eye
of anglers' tall tales and the grease
of marine engines and fry pans
this old man
this fabled wordsmith
this seasoned explorer
and salty dog
turned soldier of fortune
turned bestselling author
the bookish buccaneer
the pride of the Pulitzers
noblesse oblige of all Nobels
filled to the gills
primed with piss
vinegar and whatever
else the bar had served him
sets out in full sail
rigged out on a rugged course
guided by his own star
mapping out the illustrated
state of his own stark legend
and begins to tell stories
yarns and bold-faced lies

i offer the dead man
some beans and rice
and sweet fish
he pauses smiles
and tells me that
"a first-class meal
is as good as
a kick in the ass—
we all deserve one
once in a while"
takes my plate
and eats like
he hasn't eaten
in half a century

courage conjured up i voice
"speaking of kicks in the ass
old man, what about the time
Morley Callaghan kicked yours"
and instantly he stabs
the table with a fork
nostrils flaring eyes a rage
surging and a staged cue cut
to maniacal laughter
"you aren't much of a fisherman, boy"
he gripes rises punches the air
and fades into yachting banners
boat pictures plastic mermaids
shipping charts assorted captain's hats
and a chalkboard declaring
yesterday's soup entree and
salad bar all for fifteen ninety-five
most credit cards accepted
the old sailors and

weekend blow boaters
jostle their way up
from the patio tiki bar
brushing past
the weathered old sock
but never see him
too eager to tuck
into steaming plates of perch
and tables weighed down
with frothy beer

"did you see that?"
my finger pointing
to a laminated Lake Erie
covering cracked pressboard
"see what?"
"there, there"
there where
the old coot
disappeared
like swirling pipe smoke
and everyone
i mean everyone
sailors tourists staff
stare in amazement
at me as if i were some
solemn shore-washed wreck
or a brackish spectre
laid to waste by
a pirate's folly

and i can't believe
my good fortune
running into this old goat

here in the sobering light
of a hoary August moon
here left without a meal
the tab for want of payment
and an insatiable appetite

—a hunger
in need of
a menu

THIEF

it's what i do
in the dead of night

the wannabe prosecution
of the century

begins with this
accused on the scale

ill-fitting clothes
that must have shrunk (again)

i go for walks i say
proud in my relative disbelief
hiding the fact that
you can only walk
so far in your own home

i go for walks
watching what little
impact i am making

i go
i go for walks
you know
walking i walk you know
i go i just go and keep on going
you know how i go

i go
to the kitchen
most nights
a nocturnal pilgrimage
most sublime
where a sandwich
a cold piece of chicken
left-over something or other
sits ensconced in the cool
refrigerated madness that
waits for the hungry

i am the hungry
inspired by beveled moonlight
marking my path

i slink into the shadows
hunting for lamp-lit glory
that waits for the meek
to inherit the day-old pasta

now caught
ready for the penitential rite
or probation but never
the hunger strike
punishment cruel
and unusual

quietly i wait
to steal away
in the moment
of my return
to the dark act
of late night repast

and to chew

in silence

THE POLITICS OF VACATION

women
who sun themselves
lay exposed
to the elements
like pagan sacrifices

self-consciously
check their tops
as if they may
have misplaced
parts in their
hotel room or
at the buffet

pulling
at bikini bottoms
in constant
self-assessment
ensuring
the most
amount of
coverage

but not
at the expense
of this year's tan

SUNSET REQUIEM

i can only
imagine you
at this hour

the three of you
sitting at a table
with some wine

fruit and cheese
and stories
to share

while i consider
the quiet
lake shimmering
silver ripples
like carefully
arranged photographs

i revisit each memory
examine precise details
and discern
new meanings
from your
well-lived lives

i wonder how you are
('where' is the easy part)

i embrace this waning sun
and encourage its descent
with my silent prayer for you

and thank the
gentle genius
who designed
this moment

on beach stairs
scarred by use
this place
where i dream
in sleepless
solemnity

where i mark time
waiting by the
ever-altering shore
that changes like the
very lives forever marked
forever molded
ever-lasting and
ever sent

ON HEARING THAT A FRIEND IS DYING

someone once said
that hearing that a friend is dying
is like being hit on the head
with a two-by-four
except there isn't anyone
that i know on the face of creation
including that someone
who has survived
such a trauma

the exaggeration
is without apology
everybody knows
that it is meant only
to convey a feeling
this dark sarcasm
this numbing news
that causes heads to shake
the same ones meant
for the two-by-four
and you ask that the news be repeated
slowly because you can't believe your ears
even though there is no reason
to doubt your hearing

you feel flushed
feverish and discomforted
searching in your mind for rational thought
and the nearest bathroom to heave in

your stomach turns
the room spins
and colours become
indiscriminate

you have a how-could-this-be moment
denial becomes the favourite parlour game
and guilt becomes an unwelcome partner

we should have spent more time together
we could have—should have—done lunch
or dinner
why didn't we this
and how is it that we didn't
do that and where the hell
are the pictures from then
and when and why and why
and why and now
how preoccupied we are
with a shoe box
filled with
pictures

that should have
found themselves
in an envelope
with a note
with words
—the right words—
metaphors of hope
and joy and

now

words

carefully chosen

and crafted

with

utmost

regret

and

bitter

agony

FUNERAL FOR A POET

—for John Ditsky

the poets gather
in the chapel
the most atypical
of congregations

they take to the pews
like survivors
in rowboats
sitting their soft asses
on hard benches
surveying the others
taking deep breaths and
thinking 'it's not my turn'

a church pew is purgatory defined
an inhospitable place made all the worse by
hemorrhoids or a bad back or old age
and in the midst of their seemingly
endless discomfort
they sit and listen to the predictably
pious crap about the dearly departed
they listen even though
they secretly wish
to rise up
and shout out loud

"it's inevitable"

we all sit back and muse
we know what he would have wanted
for us to sing and dance and drink
and what would he say?
"I am really not dead—I live in my poems
and in your stories
and in the toasts you will
make when you finally get to the damned bar"

the rest of the story is left for the criticism of
lesser mortals who wait
for their turn
in wooden pews
and query

"are caskets made
from these same hard woods?"

SHOOTING SNOOKER
WITH MORDECHAI RICHLER

i would play with my jacket on
tie loosened collar unbuttoned
less authentic without a cigarette
but not being a smoker, why bluff?

surveying the table like a latter-day Napoleon
my opponent would strategize
determine with military precision his next moves
chalk the cue with the cautious eye of a sniper
and deliver the maverick blow to the billiard ball

the smoke encircling the table
loops my senses and lassoes
what remains of the oxygen
squeezed into this shabby hall
dulled by darkness i turn to light
a single swaying bulb illuminating
this icon of the loveless
this thorn in the side of division
this dean of apologia pro sua antaganismo
our glorified shit disturber

running the table as in youth
running amuck amidst the fray
pissing off the old guard
pissing into the wind
discounting their disgruntled ramblings
this bright light of his generation

swaying
flickering
casting slate-etched shadows

and delivering
with English
the final shot

on cue

ZEPPO MARX

always the straight man—
more the silent man
than one illustrious brother
(who mimed his way into immortality)

always out of place
like a nun in a brothel
or sardines on raisin bread
(something the mustached one would quip)

always the sweetheart
the one with looks and charm
a magician of sorts
(jokes slipped from your mouth and vanished)

now and forever the late man
the last to go
after the film is shot—
a pristine smile remaining
on the cutting room floor

NEIGHBOUR

—for "Island" Joe Clark

my neighbour has cancer

like an uninvited guest
it had returned
to his cottage
gone for a while
it had crossed the lake
and barged right in
like some annoying
relative or field mice
a holiday home invasion
of the worst kind

nothing changes
nothing

he hunts and fishes
he is Hiawatha
with an ATV

mud up to his ass
and he is happy
as a pig

but this cancer thing
Jesus why hit a guy
who lives life like there
is no tomorrow

there is isn't there?

he cooks up a storm
handles tools with ease
catalogues his projects
and is always doing
something
always going
somewhere
something to
be done

this is his story
beginning middle and

in the end
my neighbour
died of cancer

while planning
his next fishing trip
readying his tackle box
for the spring run

just the kind of thinking
you'd expect from someone
who thinks dying
is something
that other people do
something that
happens to neighbours
the guy across the street
celebrities and strangers

something you read
about in fiction
or the classifieds
or the small print
found on shampoo bottles

tiny and illegible

SATCHMO

in this photograph
you blow your horn
like Gabriel's descendant

eyes rolling back ecstatic
in virtuoso wonderment
despite the looming silence

you sit transfixed
only to elicit fear
from the five-year-old

who wonders why your
eyes move in the dark
in time and without music

TRILOGY: THE FAILED MUSICIAN

the mandolin weeps
in my unskilled hands again
trying for laughter

echoes in the keys
the fingers not responding
to the heart's new tune

into the juke box
letting the record do the
work i cannot do

PAPER, SCISSORS, ROCK

—for Constable John Atkinson
killed in the line of duty
May 5, 2006

what possessed you to stop
what you were doing
what made you turn left
when you should have gone right
what did you see
what did we miss
what were you thinking

to question and query
when no one saw you coming
no one saw it coming
no one knew it could happen
shouldn't happen
not here
never here

you moved as you did
as you always should
out of the darkness
into the light
a single bulb
suspended in animation
like in the movies
"where were you on the fifth of May?"
"just doing my job—just doing my..."

the hot steel of a bullet
does not discriminate
it does not disintegrate
but manages to move
with unsettling precision
regardless of race colour creed
or the myriad of apologies
that sting the heart of the hunted

the countless what ifs
wake the man-children
from their bitter
and dreamless sleep
they sit and wait
alone and accused
sit in desolation
in darkness
cold impervious solitude
walled in by their shame
shackled by their guilt
all of this because of you
your duty-bound
sense of order
noblesse oblige
with a badge

all because of you
lives remain incomplete
the road map misplaced
a journey interrupted
the compass shattered
people asking for direction
lives placed on hold
shelved suspended

because you decided
to follow your instincts
preserve and protect
to do your duty
to turn when you
could have walked away
walked the other way
the others who walk with you
the others now running
"officer down"

down when you
should have been up
watching in disbelief
utter horror
wondering what
were you thinking

on an afternoon
when risk became
a four-letter word
a board game
and a thing as remote
as a handgun
in the hands
of babes

NEXT TO LAST WORDS

my biggest fear
is failing
to finish
this

leaving it wide open
for someone
to come and complete
like it was their own

what kind of crap is this
what kind of political
machination allows
someone to come
in and claim ownership
of a phrase
some words
the syntax
and the message
that goes
with all of this

if i am dead
will someone
truly want
to finish this

will someone
really care enough
to say "hey, this guy
meant something to me

and i just want
to share this with you"

i just want to write
to create
a piece of art
something for the stage
or at the very least
a colouring book
a simple colouring book
that tells a story
with characters that
exist only
in my head
dream people who
slip between the crack
in the door or the keyhole
and vanish into molecular
heaven like some lab
experiment gone wrong

or a poem
that remains
unfinished

CLEANING UP

what was it that you said
about the famous
found dead on the toilet
like Voltaire revealed or relieved
it makes such little difference
these historical cul-de-sacs
that make up our conversation

wit sharpened by a well-read life
you re-read now with the mind's eye
in the looming darkness
measuring days by hollow sounds
disinterested comings and goings
of the walker set clopping the tiled floors
on to lunch or dinner or maybe breakfast
the meal tasteless and defined by time
and you remain
quoting the dead
in a conversation
that took place
centuries before
you were born

answering
in humble servitude
your failed scholar
ever so grateful
to have been included
at your table
with the last of the great poets

i lean to remove
the socks from the floor
fumbling with rudimentary Latin
and wishing your ancient self a sweet
good night a restful dream-dressed evening
like the young man you were
spilling coffee in a café
a lifetime or two
from the last
of this weak light